IMMIGRANT INNOVATORS

Illustrations: Calef Brown
Design: Thomas Boucher
Art Direction: Violet Lemay
Editor: Saskia Lacey

Library of Congress Cataloging-in-Publication Data available upon request.

ISBN: 978-1-950500-27-7

duopress books are available at special discounts when purchased in bulk for sales promotions as well as for fund-raising or educational use. Special editions can be created to specification. Contact us at hello@duopressbooks.com for more information.

Manufactured in Malaysia
10 9 8 7 6 5 4 3 2 1

Duo Press LLC.
8 Market Place, Suite 300
Baltimore, MD 21202
Distributed by Workman Publishing Company, Inc.
Published simultaneously in Canada by Thomas Allen & Son Limited.

To order: hello@duopressbooks.com
www.duopressbooks.com
www.workman.com

IMMIGRANT INNOVATORS

30 ENTREPRENEURS WHO MADE A DIFFERENCE

By Samantha Chagollan

Art by Calef Brown

duopress

Contents

We, the Immigrants

How many times have you heard that the United States is a nation of immigrants? Many times, for sure. What we don't hear about that often are the contributions that these immigrants bring to the country, not just in terms of culture and diversity, but also in innovation, job creation, and economic growth. Immigrants are almost twice as likely to start businesses as those born in the country. Refugees have an even higher rate of entrepreneurship. Companies owned by immigrants in the United States employ 13.5 million people.

In this book, you will read about 15 women and 15 men from 25 different countries. Some of the companies are well-known and high-tech, such as Instagram, YouTube, PayPal, and eBay. Others are more traditional, like restaurant chain Panda Express or cosmetics company Fenty Beauty. Some businesses were started when their founders wanted to bring the flavors of their native countries to the United States. These are companies like yogurt makers Chobani and Noosa. Some businesses are very big. Some are small. Like the immigrants themselves, their companies are incredibly diverse.

The stories you'll find in this book are also very varied. Take Ayah Bdeir's story, for example (on page 25). Ayah is the founder and inventor of littleBits. She wants all children to be inventors. She believes that no matter where you come from or what language you speak, you can design something great. Born to Syrian refugees in Canada, Ayah's family then moved to Lebanon, where she fell in love with electronics. Her company, littleBits, makes tiny electronic building blocks that allow kids to build their own inventions.

Building a company is not just about making money. Many of the entrepreneurs in this book worked hard to also make a difference. During the COVID-19 pandemic, immigrant innovators used their ingenuity and resources to help people in need. Mike Krieger (Instagram, page 9) used his programming expertise to build a website that tracked the way the virus was spreading in the US. Daniel Lubetzky (KIND, page 21) helped create a platform that hospitals used to request safety equipment. Rihanna (Fenty Beauty, page 35) donated millions of dollars (along with music producer Jay-Z and Twitter's Jack Dorsey) to fund COVID-19 relief efforts. Luis von Ahn (Duolingo, page 73) launched a free app to help parents homeschool young children. Chefs and activists Marcus Samuelsson (page 39) and José Andrés (page 111) turned their famous restaurants into community kitchens. They helped feed thousands of front-line workers and people in need.

No matter where you are from or what you want to do with your life, we hope this book will inspire you to get there. After all, we are all immigrants.

Mike Krieger

 *Brazil*

Cofounder of Instagram

What if you created an app used all over the world? Imagine a billion people connecting and sharing ideas with your platform. Welcome to Instagram! The famous social media app was cofounded by Mike Krieger and Kevin Systrom.

Mike was born in 1986. He grew up in São Paolo, Brazil. Even as a boy, Mike was fascinated by technology. When he was six years old, his father brought home a computer. Instantly intrigued, Mike wanted to learn everything he could about technology.

When he was 18, Mike moved to California to study at Stanford University. He earned his degree in symbolic systems. This special program mixes coding, philosophy, and psychology. Mike learned how our minds process and act on information. In essence, he learned how we use computers.

Next, Mike went to work for Meebo, an instant-messaging company. As a software engineer, he helped design Meebo's look and feel.

Mike met Kevin Systrom, his future Instagram partner, at a coffee shop in San Francisco. Soon, they were trading ideas. Kevin was developing an app that shared a user's location and photos. He asked Mike to try it.

As they exchanged ideas, Mike and Kevin became good friends.

They worked so well together, Kevin asked Mike to be cofounder of his new app.

Mike was still a Brazilian citizen. He applied for a work visa, but the approval process took a long time. Mike says, "I had moments where I was like, 'Maybe I should just tell Kevin to forget about it and find somebody else who is easier to hire.'"

It took months, but Mike finally received his visa. By then, he and Kevin had scrapped their original idea. They decided to focus on building a photo-sharing app. They had a hunch that people wanted to send photos to more than just their friends and family.

Mike and Kevin were inspired by old Polaroid pictures. The soft colors and square shape of the photos provided the design style they were going for. Mike and Kevin went to work. They built their app in just eight weeks! Soon, Instagram was ready to launch.

"INNOVATION HAPPENS BEST WHEN PEOPLE OF DIFFERENT BACKGROUNDS COME TOGETHER TO SOLVE THE WORLD'S TOUGHEST CHALLENGES."

Within two hours of going live, Instagram had so many new users that their servers crashed. The app was an enormous hit!

Today, Instagram has more than one billion active users each month. Mike and Kevin sold Instagram to Facebook for $1 billion in 2012. Now, Instagram's worth is estimated to be 100 times that.

NATIVE TONGUE
As a kid, Mike and his family moved frequently because of his dad's work. He has lived in Portugal, Argentina, and the United States. Mike knows English, Portuguese, and countless computer languages!

In 2013, President Barack Obama mentioned Mike in a speech about immigrants who are successful and help the US economy. "Instagram was started with the help of an immigrant who studied here and stayed here," said President Obama. "Right now in one of those classrooms there's a student wrestling with how to turn their big idea...into a big business."

QUICK START
When Instagram launched, 10,000 people downloaded the app within a few hours. By the end of the first week, the count was 200,000 users. In the beginning, Mike and Kevin did all the work themselves. As time passed, they hired a few employees to help them, but they kept the team small.

Instagram has grown into something infinitely bigger than Mike or Kevin dreamed. Mike still loves that people can use Instagram to "travel" around the world, discovering new places and making new friends.

Andrew & Peggy Cherng

China   Myanmar

Founders of Panda Express

All over America, people enjoy fried rice, stir-fry, and orange chicken from Panda Express. The hugely successful Chinese-food franchise was founded by Andrew and Peggy Cherng. Their story starts on the other side of the world.

Born in China, Andrew grew up in Japan, where his father worked as a chef. Peggy was born in Myanmar but was raised in Hong Kong. Both moved to America for college. When they met at Baker University in Kansas, Peggy was studying electrical engineering. Andrew was earning his degree in math.

The couple fell in love, got married, and moved to Los Angeles. In 1973, Andrew and his father started a small restaurant called the Panda Inn. Running the business was a family affair. Andrew's father was the restaurant's chef, and his mother cooked rice and washed dishes. Andrew handled everything else.

Business was slow at first, but the Cherng family was determined to succeed. Slowly but surely, the number of customers grew. Once Panda Inn became successful, Peggy joined the team. She quit her job coding simulators for the US Navy to run the restaurant's back office. It was a big gamble!

Panda Inn's next growth spurt came from an unlikely source. A customer who owned a local mall asked the Cherngs if they would like to open a smaller version of their restaurant in the food court. Andrew and Peggy opened the first Panda Express at the Glendale Galleria mall in 1983.

Peggy used her technical skills to give their new business an edge. She tracked data on what was selling and made changes as Panda Express grew. Her efforts paid off—the restaurant was a big success! Within a decade, Panda Express had more than 100 restaurants across the country.

ORANGE YOU GLAD YOU KNOW?
Panda Express has served 80 million pounds of their most popular dish— orange chicken— since 2016. The recipe was created in 1987 by head chef Andy Kao and remains top secret.

As time passed, the company continued to grow, adding more locations every year. Today, Panda Express has an innovation kitchen, where new ideas—like orange chicken wraps and boba tea—are put to the test.

As Panda Express expanded, Andrew and Peggy reminded their family that every employee mattered. From the start, the Cherngs put their workers first, investing in the growth of their employees. They opened the University of Panda, where workers can learn everything from self-defense to public speaking.

WHAT THE CHORK?

In 2016, Panda Express introduced the "chork," a clever combination of a fork and chopsticks. The utensil was designed to be a bridge between Chinese and American cultures.

In 1999, Andrew and Peggy founded a charity group called Panda Cares. "Our belief is that everything comes down to character," said Peggy. "If we can develop strong culture for our young children, they can conquer anything."

Panda Cares has raised more than $100 million for children's health and education. Most of this money came from customers! Donation boxes in Panda Express restaurants have collected over $90 million. The Cherngs have also raised money for wildfire and disaster relief. In total, the Panda Cares charity has raised more than $140 million.

Each meal at Panda Express ends with a fortune cookie. Here's a sample saying: "Life's greatest joys come from sharing good food." Through their restaurants, the Cherngs have spread joy all over the world!

"THE RESTAURANT BUSINESS IS THE PEOPLE BUSINESS, AND PEOPLE ARE OUR INVESTMENT."
—PEGGY CHERNG

Ruzwana Bashir

🏴 *England*

Cofounder of Peek

Everyone loves a vacation. But what do we love? Often, it's the people we meet, the food we eat, and the fun things we do.

That's what Ruzwana Bashir believes, and it's why she cofounded Peek.

It all started with her birthday. Ruzwana was planning a weekend trip to Istanbul, Turkey, with her friends. She wanted to find memorable activities for the group. She spent more than 20 hours looking up activities, asking friends for ideas, and paging through travel guides. The process of planning the trip was ridiculous! It was taking Ruzwana more time to plan the trip than she would actually be on the trip.

Ruzwana thought, "Wouldn't it be great if you could have a one-stop shop where you could discover what to do when you travel and then actually book it?" She didn't know it at the time, but she had found her calling. Ruzwana would build an easy place for travelers to find fun and unusual experiences.

Ruzwana grew up in Yorkshire, England, in a traditional Muslim household. Her parents were from Pakistan, and her father worked long days running a market stall to provide for the family.

While hard work was expected of the young girl, school was not a priority. Nonetheless, Ruzwana loved to learn and rose to the top of her classes.

When a teacher suggested she apply to Oxford, Ruzwana did. She kept it a secret from her parents until she was accepted. "In a family like mine, the whole idea of letting your daughter go away to university is a huge deal." Happily, Ruzwana's parents let her go because it was such a well-known school.

FAST FACTS: ENGLAND
Official Name: England
Capital: London
Population: 56 million
Official Language: None
Currency: Pound sterling
Area: 50,301 square miles

Heading for Oxford, Ruzwana planned to become a doctor. Once she arrived in Oxford, everything changed. She saw the world in a new way. For the first time, Ruzwana stopped wearing her traditional clothing and head scarf. She cut her hair, wore jeans, and focused her studies on politics, philosophy, and economics.

GRIT IS GOOD
Ruzwana has said that while her childhood wasn't always easy, it helped her find the success she has now. "What I went through growing up prepared me well for entrepreneurship," she says. "I had to fight for a lot of things and I developed a grit that has really paid off."

"I was always the explorer, the person that didn't have any limits—I still don't," says Ruzwana. "I'd always had a passion and knew I wanted to be an entrepreneur and build something from scratch."

Ruzwana became the second Asian female president of the Oxford Union debating society. After graduation, she moved to the United States to work at financial giant Goldman Sachs. Soon after, Ruzwana became the first woman on her team at Blackstone Group, another financial hub.

After a few years, Ruzwana was ready for a new challenge. She pursued a graduate degree, a master's of business administration, at Harvard University.

It was during this time that Ruzwana planned the life-changing trip to Istanbul that inspired Peek. With her cofounder, Oskar Bruening, she created her one-stop travel shop. Investors helped Peek launch in 2012.

The travel company offers everything from treehouse ziplining in Oregon to walking photography tours of London. No matter where you want to go in the world, there is probably a Peek experience to make it better.

"We've all been taught that buying things—that expensive handbag or that new house—is going to make us happy; it doesn't," says Ruzwana. "But there's evidence that buying an experience makes us 50 percent happier than buying a product. We can create special memories with people that we care about, learn, be inspired, be enthralled and engage our curiosity."

"WOULDN'T IT BE AMAZING IF WE SPENT AS MUCH ENERGY INVESTING IN EXPERIENCES AS WE DO INVESTING IN THINGS?"

Daniel Lubetzky

Mexico

Founder of KIND Snacks

Daniel Lubetzky has always wanted one thing: to make the world a kinder place.

Daniel learned the importance of kindness from his father, Roman Lubetzky. Roman was a Holocaust survivor. He was freed from the Dachau concentration camp in Germany when he was just 15 years old. Once liberated, Roman settled in Mexico. There, he met and married a woman named Sonia—Daniel's mother.

Born in 1968, Daniel was raised in Mexico City. He grew up listening to painful stories about his father's time in the concentration camp. Despite the terrible suffering Roman endured, he told Daniel it was the kindness of others that helped him survive.

When Daniel was 16, his family immigrated to Texas. There, the teenager found a creative way to earn extra cash. He bought cheap watches and sold them at a markup. Daniel also sold trinkets at local flea markets. He quickly discovered he had a talent for making money!

During college, Daniel wrote his thesis on how smart business practices could help in the Arab-Israeli conflict. His idea was to reward American businesses that worked with companies in both Israel and Arab countries, uniting them in a common cause. If two groups with different ideas could cooperate, anything was possible!

Daniel's passion for making the world a better place led him to Stanford Law School. He ended up more frustrated than inspired. The young man wasn't sure how to make the world better, but he knew that he had to find a way.

Founding PeaceWorks was Daniel's next adventure. His new company created a sundried tomato spread by sourcing ingredients from Arab and Israeli companies that wouldn't usually cooperate. Big success! Each business profited from their common cause.

On a work trip for PeaceWorks, Daniel searched for a healthy snack bar but couldn't find what he wanted. All the bars looked the same—gooey and tasteless. He couldn't even pronounce most of the ingredients on the wrappers!

Daniel had a vision for a new type of snack bar, one made of tasty, whole ingredients that you could see through the wrapper. His bars would be different: delicious, good for you, and powered by kindness.

In 2004, KIND Snacks, Daniel's wholesome

ONE-MAN SHOW
When he started KIND Snacks, Daniel did all the jobs—it was just him! He was CEO, salesman, box packer, and delivery guy too.

"KINDNESS IS CONTAGIOUS."

treats, hit the market. They weren't an overnight success. "It's really important that if you're pursuing your own dreams you don't give up too early," he explained. After years of trying different ingredients and packaging, KIND Snacks took off.

Today, KIND Snacks employs hundreds of people. Two billion snack bars have been sold worldwide.

Over the years, Daniel has had many successes, but he is most proud of the role kindness plays in his company's culture. The KIND Movement has inspired people to spread more than 17 million acts of kindness around the world, from making care kits for foster kids to building showers for the homeless.

"Kind is a powerful word," says Daniel. "I don't try to live up to being The Kind Guy. I strive, but I'm as imperfect as anybody. Still, the name of the company makes me want to aspire to something."

RAISING THE BAR
During the COVID-19 pandemic of 2020, the KIND Foundation partnered with other companies to coordinate resources for hospitals and other health-care institutions. Daniel also committed to providing a minimum of 5 million KIND bars to health-care and other front-line workers.

Ayah Bdeir

 *Lebanon*

Founder and Inventor of littleBits

When you think of an inventor, what comes to mind? Do you imagine an old man with wild hair hunched over a set of bubbling beakers? According to Ayah Bdeir, "Inventors come in all shapes and sizes, all ages, all backgrounds. They speak all languages and come from all countries."

Ayah moved around a lot when she was young. Her parents were Syrian refugees. Ayah was born in Canada in 1982. When she was still young, her family moved again—this time to Lebanon. Ayah grew up in Lebanon and considers herself Lebanese.

As a young girl, Ayah was fascinated with electronics. She adored playing with home chemistry kits and electricity sets. Ayah's parents encouraged her passions. They gave her a computer, which she used to make greeting cards and posters. These were her first attempts at programming!

As a teenager, Ayah dreamed of going to MIT, a school for engineers in the United States. She applied repeatedly but was not accepted. Eventually, Ayah earned a degree in computer engineering in Lebanon. After graduating, she applied to MIT again. This time, Ayah got in! She joined the famous MIT Media Lab and earned her master's degree.

After MIT, Ayah worked as a teacher, researcher, and presenter.

"INVENTION IS A PROCESS THAT ANYONE CAN LEARN."

It was during this time that she invented something wonderful— tiny electronic building blocks. The color-coded pieces made it easy to tell which blocks snapped together. The blocks, called littleBits, were perfect for kids who wanted to invent and build their own contraptions.

Ayah took a prototype of her building blocks to trade shows. Children loved creating gizmos with her unique toys! They asked a ton of questions. She was inspired by their enthusiasm.

WORD OF WISDOM
Ayah says her favorite word in Arabic is *kazdoura*. She says, "It means taking a walk or a drive...but it implies a deeper connection with someone or a place."

Ayah dreamed of children everywhere playing with her electronic blocks. In 2011, she founded littleBits with the goal of helping more kids learn about technology—especially girls!

Children used Ayah's creation to build all kinds of machines: bubble blowers, musical instruments, even a sibling alarm!

INSPIRING INVENTIONS
littleBits has partnered with 20,000 schools around the globe. More than a million inventions have been created using Ayah's building blocks.

A few months after the company launched, Ayah discovered a YouTube video of a boy building a littleBits machine with his dad.

Could there be more videos? Ayah searched. She was delighted to discover that kids were using her building blocks all over the world. There were videos from Mexico, South Africa, Canada, and Singapore.

Ayah wants all children to be inventors. She believes that no matter where you come from or what language you speak, you can design something great.

As she looks to the future, Ayah hopes that kids keep inventing and learning about engineering. "Whether you want to be in fashion or you want to be in art, or space science, or robotics, or writing, engineering can be a useful tool to inform how you think and how you learn, and how you expand your horizons."

WORK OF ART

The Museum of Modern Art in New York City made littleBits part of its permanent collection.

FAST FACTS: LEBANON

Official Name: Lebanese Republic
Capital: Beirut
Population: 7 million
Official Language: Arabic
Currency: Lebanese pound
Area: 4,036 square miles

AWARD WINNER

In 2019, Ayah was named one of the BBC's 100 Women. The list celebrates the most inspiring and influential women in the world. A few years earlier, *Popular Mechanics* called Ayah one of the 25 Makers Who Are Reinventing the American Dream.

Immigrant Entrepreneurs: By the Numbers

Immigrants and their children have founded amazing companies all across America. These are businesses like Apple, PepsiCo, Ford Motor Company, Facebook, and the Walt Disney Company.

They are called New American companies because they were founded by people new to the United States. The following New American businesses are the best of the best. Each is hugely successful!

TOP 500 COMPANIES IN AMERICA

A 2019 study showed that nearly 45% of the country's most profitable companies were founded by immigrants or their children. These companies employ millions of people.

45%

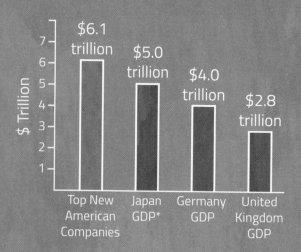

New American companies fuel our economy. They create more wealth each year than some countries!

*GDP stands for gross domestic product; it is the value of all goods and services produced by a country.

New American companies are all over the United States. This map shows just a few New American companies.

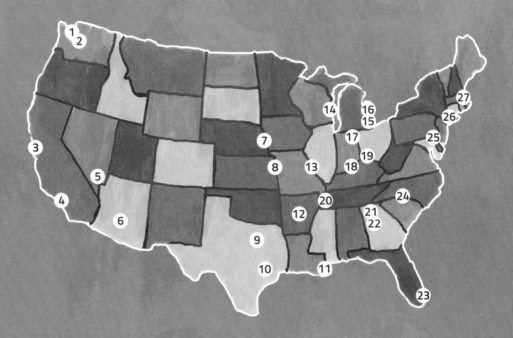

1 Washington, Amazon.com
2 Washington, Costco Wholesale
3 California, Apple
4 California, the Walt Disney Company
5 Nevada, Las Vegas Sands
6 Arizona, Avnet
7 Nebraska, Kiewit Corporation
8 Kansas, Seaboard
9 Texas, AT&T
10 Texas, Sysco
11 Louisiana, Entergy
12 Arkansas, Windstream Holdings
13 Missouri, Emerson Electric
14 Wisconsin, Kohl's
15 Michigan, Ford Motor Company
16 Michigan, Lear
17 Indiana, Steel Dynamics
18 Kentucky, Yum Brands
19 Ohio, Procter & Gamble
20 Tennessee, International Paper
21 Georgia, Home Depot
22 Georgia, United Parcel Service (UPS)
23 Florida, AutoNation
24 North Carolina, Bank of America
25 Delaware, DuPont
26 New York, Verizon Communications
27 Massachusetts, General Electric

Steve Chen & Jawed Karim

🇹🇼 *Taiwan*　　📗 *Germany*

Cofounders of YouTube

Can you even imagine a world without YouTube? With more than two billion monthly users worldwide, YouTube is truly everywhere. It's the first place you go to watch videos about pretty much anything.

Once upon a time, YouTube was just an idea shared by three friends. Cofounders Steve Chen, Jawed Karim, and Chad Hurley were looking for a way to meet girls. That's right—YouTube started out as a dating app! The idea was for singles to learn more about each other by creating and sharing personal videos.

YouTube's cofounders met while working at PayPal, but their stories began in different countries. Chad was born in America. Steve and Jawed came from overseas.

Steve Chen was born in Taiwan in 1978 and moved to the United States as a child. He was an outstanding math and computer science student. Early in high school, Steve took the SAT. His score earned him a spot at the Illinois Mathematics Science Academy. Steve flourished at his new high school. He was excited to work with state-of-the-art computers and be surrounded by like-minded students.

Thousands of miles away, Jawed Karim was growing up in Germany.

He was born in 1979, just a year after Steve. Jawed's mother was a biochemist, and his father was a researcher. In 1992, the family moved to Saint Paul, Minnesota. Later, Jawed studied computer science at the University of Illinois.

Steve and Jawed were hired at PayPal, where they met Chad Hurley. All three young men were interested in the idea of sharing videos online. When the dating project didn't work, they quickly shifted their energy to a bigger idea. Their new goal was simply to share personal videos. YouTube was born!

Jawed uploaded the first video, "Me at the Zoo," to YouTube in 2005. Only 18 seconds long, the clip features Jawed standing in front of an elephant exhibit, talking about what he sees. Today, Jawed's first video has more than 83 million views.

WHO'S WATCHING
Over 100 countries around the world use YouTube. The site is accessed in 80 different languages. YouTubers watch one billion hours of videos every single day! Most viewers are between the ages of 18 and 34, and more than 70% watch on their mobile phones.

YouTube became an enormous success. Steve, Jawed, and Chad watched as users uploaded thousands of videos. In the first year, millions of people visited the site! Soon, Google offered to buy YouTube for $1.65 billion. The three cofounders agreed to the sale and instantly became multimillionaires.

Steve believes that entrepreneurs should gamble on new ideas. He says, "It's important to take risks if you do decide to launch your own company. You must be courageous enough to make pivotal decisions that can alter your company's path."

Steve, Jawed, and Chad's gamble changed everything. What began as a dating site became a hub for entertainment, culture, and social connection. Users come to YouTube to teach, learn, and vent. The website has turned regular people into superstars. YouTube has changed our world.

"IF OTHER ENGINEERS AND SCIENTISTS—ESPECIALLY YOUNG PROFESSIONALS—CONTINUED TO INNOVATE ON THEIR OWN, THERE'S NO TELLING WHAT TRANSFORMATIVE TECHNOLOGIES THEY COULD CREATE." —STEVE CHEN

Rihanna

Barbados

Singer, Actress, and Founder of Fenty Beauty

Pop star, fashion icon, and actress, Rihanna is one of the world's most famous people. But before fame came knocking, she was just a little girl from Barbados.

Growing up in the Caribbean, Robyn Rihanna Fenty loved to sing. Born in 1988, home life wasn't always easy for Rihanna, and music was the perfect escape. When she was 15, Rihanna competed in a beauty pageant and sang Mariah Carey's "Hero." She won the competition!

That same year, Rihanna formed a musical group with two classmates. When the trio learned a record producer was vacationing nearby, they were determined to meet him. The girls managed to score an audition. Rihanna's star power was undeniable. The producer says, "The minute Rihanna walked into the room, it was like the two other girls didn't exist."

Rihanna was only 16 when she moved to the United States to record a demo album. "When I left Barbados, I didn't look back," she says. "I wanted to do what I had to do, even if it meant moving to America."

Rap superstar Jay-Z gave Rihanna her big break. He asked her to sing for him. Rihanna had never been more nervous, but she found courage in the moment. She says, "I remember staring into everybody's eyes in the room while I was singing, and at that point, I was fearless." Jay-Z signed her to the record label on the spot.

Rihanna's musical career took off. She released one hit song after another. She sold millions of albums and won Grammy and MTV awards. In 2015, Rihanna became the first artist in history with 100 million song downloads. Her songs include "Umbrella," "Disturbia," "Diamonds," and "We Found Love."

In 2016, the famous singer took a left turn. Just when fans were expecting her next chart-smashing hit, Rihanna chose a different path. She debuted her clothing line Fenty x Puma at New York Fashion Week. Her new business became a huge success.

Rihanna didn't stop there. She launched Fenty Beauty the next year. The revolutionary makeup line offers 40 different shades of foundation. Other companies only offer a handful of shades. Rihanna wanted to create cosmetics for every skin tone.

Fenty Beauty ads feature diverse models—all shapes, sizes, and skin tones are represented. The company is adored for its mission to celebrate all women. Rihanna says, "Some are finding their shade of foundation for the first time, getting emotional at the counter. That's something I will never get over."

GIVING BACK

In 2012, Rihanna started the Clara Lionel Foundation, named after her grandparents. The foundation focuses on disaster relief and education, especially in the Caribbean. When Hurricane Dorian landed in 2019, it was the strongest hurricane to hit the Bahamas. The foundation donated $1 million to help the 70,000 people in need.

In its first month, Fenty Beauty appeared in over a thousand stores around the world. The company earned close to $100 million! In 2017, Fenty Beauty was chosen by *Time Magazine* as one of the year's best inventions.

Fenty Beauty made nearly $570 million in its first year. Since the company's launch, Rihanna has started her own fashion line in partnership with LVMH, a luxury goods group. This makes her the first black woman to lead her own luxury fashion house.

Rihanna has no plans to stop dreaming and creating the world she wants to live in. But no matter what, she will always come back to music. "Music is like, speaking in code to the world...Me the designer, me the woman who creates makeup—it all started with music. It was my first pen pal-ship to the world...All of these other things flourish on top of that foundation."

FAST FACTS: BARBADOS
Official Name: Barbados
Capital: Bridgetown
Population: 285,400
Official Language: English
Currency: Barbados dollar
Area: 166 square miles

IN THE NAVY
Rihanna calls her diehard fans the Navy. On social media, these fans are referred to as #RihannaNavy. Rihanna's biggest fans proudly say that the singer is their inspiration in all things.

CALL ME ROBYN
The world knows her as Rihanna. Over 79 million people follow her on Instagram as @badgalriri. But friends and family still call her by her birth name: Robyn.

Marcus Samuelsson

Ethiopia

Chef, Author, and Activist

Marcus Samuelsson is one of the most famous chefs in the world. He owns more than two dozen restaurants, and his cookbooks have inspired many.

Life did not start easy for Marcus. Born in Ethiopia in 1970, his mother contracted tuberculosis when he was still a baby. When she died, Marcus and his sister were adopted by a family in Sweden.

It was in his Swedish grandmother's kitchen that Marcus learned to cook. Helga loved making jam from lingonberries, blueberries, and apples. She also made delicious roasted chicken, meatballs, and ginger snaps and other cookies.

Marcus went fishing every morning with his father and uncles. They caught mackerel, crayfish, and even lobsters. The young boy grew up loving fresh, local food. When he was 16, Marcus began studying cooking seriously.

In 1989, Marcus graduated from the Culinary Institute in Gothenburg, Sweden. He traveled to Switzerland, and then France, to learn more about food preparation at some of the finest restaurants in the world.

When Marcus was 22, he immigrated to the United States. He landed a job at Aquavit, a Scandinavian restaurant in New York City.

Over time, Marcus worked his way up the culinary ranks. Eventually, he was offered the position of executive chef. Marcus was nervous about his new job.

"It's a famous restaurant," he said. "I didn't want to be the guy to close it."

Marcus was so talented, everyone began to notice. The *New York Times* gave him a three-star review, one of the highest awards for chefs. Marcus was the youngest chef to earn the rating.

More prizes followed. Marcus was making his dreams come true. In 2006, while biking through New York's Harlem neighborhood, a new dream dawned. Marcus fell in love with the community. He imagined opening a restaurant that showcased Harlem's food, culture, and history.

As Marcus's success grew, so did his ambition. In 2009, he was invited to cook dinner for President Barack Obama at the White

AND THE AWARD GOES TO...
In 1999, Marcus was awarded the Rising Chef Award from the James Beard Foundation. This is one of the highest honors a chef can achieve. In 2003, Marcus was awarded Best Chef: New York City by the same organization.

"HARD WORK IS ITS OWN REWARD. INTEGRITY IS PRICELESS. ART DOES FEED THE SOUL."

House. At previous state banquets, chefs had prepared French cuisine. Marcus dared to do something different. Because the dinner was in honor of the prime minister of India, the young chef prepared Indian food.

Using herbs and vegetables from the White House garden, Marcus created delicious vegetarian dishes. The president and his guests feasted on red lentil soup, green curry prawns, and roasted potato dumplings. The dinner was a hit!

Soon after, Marcus made his biggest dream come true. He opened his own restaurant, Red Rooster Harlem. Marcus brought to life the food he loved, with American dishes that hinted at his Swedish and African roots. His greatest goal for Red Rooster was "to be a place where people from all walks of life break bread together."

Marcus went on to open dozens of restaurants and write four cookbooks. He was the winner of *Top Chef Masters*, earning $115,000 for UNICEF. Marcus has appeared on many cooking shows, including *Iron Chef*, *Chopped*, and *Chopped Junior*.

In 2013, Marcus wrote a memoir called *Yes, Chef*. In the book, Marcus describes his incredible journey. He says, "One of the things I have learned during the time I have spent in the United States is an old African-American saying: Each one, teach one. I want to believe that I am here to teach one and, more, that there is one here who is meant to teach me. And if we each one teach one, we will make a difference."

CRISIS RESPONSE
Marcus and his team turned his New York and New Jersey restaurants into "community kitchens" during the COVID-19 pandemic. They offered free meals to thousands of residents. He also partnered with José Andrés (page 111) to deliver free meals to people in need.

Mariam Naficy

Iran

Founder of Minted

When Mariam Naficy left Iran with her family in 1979, she was just nine years old. A violent revolution had forced her family to flee the country. She had to leave almost everything behind.

After fleeing Iran, Mariam's family moved to the United States, and then again to Egypt. When she was 14, they finally settled in America.

It wasn't easy fitting in at school. Mariam felt like an outsider, but she didn't let the experience break her spirit. "I decided I had to not let other people define me," says Mariam. "I had to figure out how to cope on my own."

She grew from her early struggles and thrived as a student. Mariam graduated from college and then went on to study business at Stanford. She started her first business right away, an online cosmetics company called Eve. The company was a big success! In the first year, Mariam's business made $10 million. She later sold Eve for $100 million.

Celebrating her success, Mariam took time off to travel with her husband. But soon, she was ready to get back to work.

"I was captivated by the idea of bloggers," says Mariam. "These unknown writers were coming from nowhere, were unaffiliated with big institutions, but people wanted to read their work."

She thought the same idea could work with artists. Surely there were talented designers just waiting to be discovered. Maybe the internet was the way to make the connection!

Mariam launched Minted in 2008. The website encouraged unknown artists to submit their designs online. Then, people could vote for the designs they liked best. The most popular designs would be printed on greeting cards, and the artists would earn money from the sales.

When the company first started, it also sold products from established stationery brands. But these products weren't selling well. Mariam noticed that customers tended to buy the designs they had voted on. She realized that customers liked being a part of the process. By voting for their favorites, they became cheerleaders for their favorite designs.

START SMALL

Minted's first challenge was in 2008. The competition received only 66 designs. Today, tens of thousands of designs have been entered into Minted challenges. Winning designs are sold online and in stores like West Elm and Target.

GROUP EFFORT

Crowdsourcing uses the insight and ideas of many people to solve a problem. The phrase first showed up in 2006, when Jeff Howe, an editor at *Wired* magazine, used the word to describe how people outside of a company can contribute to its success.

"When we started posting the winners of our first crowdsourced-design challenge, sales started to slowly trickle in," says Mariam.

The company began to grow. More and more designers and customers joined the Minted community. Mariam learned as the company grew, making small changes along the way. The first time Minted offered holiday cards created by Minted artists, she says they "blew out the doors."

Mariam knew she had created a valuable community. She says, "I really love the artists and the designers and I really wanted to bring their work to the world."

Today, there are more than 15,000 artists on Minted. Customers have bought hundreds of millions of dollars worth of designs.

You can still vote on and buy greeting cards at Minted. But you can also find all kinds of other treasures, from wall art to murals and pillows. The most popular artists have their own online shops featuring their designs.

With Minted, Mariam has created a beautiful way for unknown artists to share their work with the world.

FRIENDLY FEEDBACK
Minted artists can choose to receive feedback from their peers and make changes to their designs before submitting them for voting. Those that receive feedback score 25% higher in competitions on average. This feature of the Minted community has helped foster friendships between artists.

"ENTREPRENEURSHIP IS NOT JUST MY WORK, IT IS MY HOBBY. I LOVE IT."

Hamdi Ulukaya

 *Turkey*

Founder of Chobani

Have you ever tried Greek yogurt? If you have, it's probably partly thanks to Hamdi Ulukaya.

Hamdi was born in 1972. He grew up in a small village in Turkey, near the Kurdish mountains. His family owned a dairy farm where they raised sheep and goats. They also made cheese and yogurt.

When Hamdi grew up, he studied political science at Ankara University in Turkey. As a student, Hamdi was interested in Kurdish rights. He attended political demonstrations and wrote opinions for a newspaper. One day Hamdi was arrested.

The police let him go with a warning. Hamdi believed his life would never be the same. Fearing for his safety, he left Turkey.

Although Hamdi had never planned on immigrating to the United States, his goals changed. In 1994, he arrived in New York with just $3,000 and a small suitcase. Hamdi knew little English and didn't have any friends in America. Despite his disadvantages, Hamdi didn't give up. He studied hard. In time, Hamdi attended New York's Adelphi University, focusing on English and business.

Two years later, his father visited. When Hamdi went grocery shopping for food his father liked, he was disappointed with the local market's cheese selection. The cheeses had little flavor and were very different than the cheese Hamdi's family made. His father suggested that Hamdi make his own cheese to sell in the US.

Hamdi wasn't sure if he wanted to mimic his family's Turkish cheese. However, he lived in the perfect place for dairy farming. Hamdi's home in Troy, New York, was close to many farms. Why not give it a try?

Hamdi imported some of his family's cheeses from Turkey and sold them. In 2005, he discovered that a local yogurt and cheese factory was for sale. When Hamdi visited, he noticed more than the building. He saw the workers too. They would lose their jobs if the company shut down.

Taking out a small business loan, Hamdi bought the old factory. He kept as many of the original employees as he could. Together, they built a Greek yogurt business. Chobani was different than other yogurts on the market.

In a typical American business, the chief executive officer (CEO) makes most of the profit. Hamdi wanted Chobani to be unique. He didn't want to focus on making money for himself. Hamdi wanted to put his employees first.

"IT'S YOUR EMPLOYEES YOU TAKE CARE OF FIRST, NOT THE PROFITS."

"Chobani" comes from the Turkish word *çoban*, which means "shepherd." You can tell Hamdi was thinking about his childhood when he named his business!

Chobani makes a point to pay its workers well. In 2016, Hamdi was able to offer employees shares of the company. He said, "The staff was always proud, but this ownership piece was missing. This is probably the smartest, most tactical thing you can do for a company." Hamdi calls this "the new way of business."

What happened was incredible! Chobani grew and grew—Hamdi hired hundreds of workers. Today, the amazing company is worth $2 billion. It is the top-selling Greek yogurt brand in the United States.

Chobani's employees earn twice the minimum wage. A remarkable 30% are refugees. According to Hamdi, "My goal at Chobani was not to build just a product, but to build a culture...to build tomorrow's company."

Now, Hamdi is taking his powerful new ideas to the rest of the business world. In 2019, he gave a TED Talk called "The Anti-CEO Playbook." Hamdi explained the importance of giving back to employees. "You have to lead by example," he said. "Chobani can inspire a new way of business, a new way of work, a new way of innovation."

GOT YOGURT?
Yogurt has been a part of Middle Eastern, European, and Indian diets for centuries, but it's fairly new to Americans. Plain yogurt was first sold in the US in the 1940s. A decade later, the company Dannon added sugars, fruits, and flavors to make it more appetizing to Americans. By the '70s, Americans loved yogurt, and in the '80s, frozen yogurt became a huge craze.

Max Levchin

■ Ukraine

Cofounder of PayPal

Imagine you're a kid who loves math so much that it's all you ever think about. Then, when you're ten years old, you learn how to program on your mom's computer. You discover you love computers even more than math!

This kid was Max Levchin. He was born in Ukraine in 1975. Growing up, Max rarely had access to a computer. This didn't stop him from learning how to program! Max wrote tons of computer games by hand. He spent hours on park benches writing programs in notebooks. Examining the code, Max would often rewrite games to make them more efficient.

When Max was 16, his family moved to America. On the plane, he discovered a computer magazine. Flipping through the pages, Max spotted a computer for $650. "How much money do we have?" he asked his mother. "We have $733 for the entire family," she told him. "It's all we have."

Max's computer would have to wait. In Chicago, he enjoyed attending his new American school. He refined his accent watching sitcoms and the news on a broken TV rescued from the trash.

Max went to college at the University of Illinois, where he studied computer science and cryptology. It was the study of cryptology, or secure data storage, that made Max a millionaire.

"I kept on starting companies on campus, and they just kept on failing," says Max. "Four companies, in the span of three years... But I loved starting them up, coming up with one hare-brained business idea after another. And they just kept. on. failing."

After graduating, Max moved to Silicon Valley. In 1998, the dot-com boom was in full swing. Young computer scientists were making their fortunes founding tech companies. Max couldn't wait to join their ranks.

FLEEING DISASTER
Max first left Kiev as a child, after the Chernobyl nuclear accident. His home in Kiev was only 90 miles away from the nuclear plant. Max's parents knew they had to get their son as far away from the radiation as they could. They put Max on a train and sent him 1,000 miles south to Crimea.

One morning, he attended a lecture by Peter Thiel. Peter often invested in new companies, and Max wanted to meet him. After the lecture, they went to breakfast and Max pitched two ideas. Peter loved one of them.

That idea became PayPal, the world's first virtual system for exchanging money. In 1999, Max launched the business with several cofounders. PayPal's most famous cofounder is Elon Musk. Like Max, Elon is an immigrant. He was born in South Africa. Today, Elon is best known as the multibillionaire CEO of Tesla Motors.

PayPal became a household name. It was

seen as a safe and simple way for people to pay each other online. Max is credited with developing the anti-fraud technology that makes the service so appealing.

In 2002, Max and his cofounders sold the company to eBay for $1.5 billion. He used his share of the profits to invest in other companies.

PAY IT FORWARD
Max has invested in more than 100 startup companies, including Yelp. He strongly believes in helping other immigrant entrepreneurs on their journeys to success. Max says, "My story isn't unique—America is a nation of immigrants and has always been a magnet for strivers, innovators, and entrepreneurs from every corner of the globe."

Today, Max is founder and CEO of Affirm, an online lending service that works like a virtual credit card. He is still programming and innovating—and still wants to help others. "We're here to improve lives, if that means more work for us, or that we make less money, we will always take the more difficult path in favor of treating people better."

"I BELIEVE THAT THE MOST PROMISING ENTREPRENEURS FROM AROUND THE WORLD SHOULD HAVE THE SAME OPPORTUNITY I HAD—THE CHANCE TO DELIVER ON THEIR POTENTIAL, HERE IN AMERICA."

Shan-Lyn Ma

🇦🇺 *Australia*

Cofounder and CEO of Zola

Some little girls dream of becoming teachers, doctors, or astronauts. Shan-Lyn Ma imagined something different. She dreamed of working at a big American internet company.

Shan-Lyn was born in Singapore in 1977, but her family soon moved to Sydney, Australia. Growing up in Australia, she dreamed of pursuing her education in the United States.

"Even though I didn't have much growing up, I was told if you work hard, then you can do anything," says Shan-Lyn. "I dreamed about changing the world, creating something big out of nothing."

From an early age, Shan-Lyn had a passion for technology. She idolized Jerry Yang, the cofounder of Yahoo. Shan-Lyn admired his drive and achievements. Jerry was an immigrant who had become immensely successful. She hoped to someday work for him in the States.

Big dreams require dedication. But Shan-Lyn knew how to work hard. During college, she supported herself with three jobs.

When Shan-Lyn graduated, she moved to California to earn her master's degree in business at Stanford University. After college, she landed her dream job at Yahoo. Finally, she was working at Jerry Yang's company! Shan-Lyn put her usual outstanding effort into the new job. Soon, she was promoted at Yahoo.

While Shan-Lyn worked hard to succeed, her friends were getting married seemingly every weekend! She didn't enjoy the chore of shopping for wedding gifts. Why was it so hard to find a present?

Most engaged couples used a registry, a list of gifts for their wedding. Shan-Lyn thought registries were complicated and impersonal. Wasn't there a better way to select presents? She talked to her recently married friend, Nobu Nakaguchi. He agreed that wedding registries were awful and stressful to create. The two friends put their heads together and came up with something better.

Zola was born! It was an innovative wedding site offering everything a couple could need. The website's tools helped couples plan their wedding and provided options for guests to give cash or add to a couple's honeymoon fund. It was a new way of giving gifts.

PARTNER POWER
Shan-Lyn and Nobu Nakaguchi, her business partner, believe it's important to stay connected. They spend at least 10 minutes together every day. Whether they step out of the office for a quick coffee or power lunch, they chat about new ideas, solve problems, or just catch up on each other's lives.

Within six years, Zola became the fastest-growing wedding registry business in the United States. Shan-Lyn and Nobu's company is worth $600 million. Today, Zola has even more tools. Couples can create their own website for free, plan out wedding details, or even design their own invitations. Recently, the company opened a retail store in New York City.

Shan-Lyn isn't stopping. She has bigger dreams for Zola's future. Shan-Lyn wants to help couples even after their wedding. More helpful resources for newlyweds are on the way.

Shan-Lyn has never forgotten the country she calls home. Each year, Zola celebrates Australia Day. "It's one of my favorite days of the year!" she says.

With Zola, Shan-Lyn Ma created her own fairy tale. She built a big American internet company.

"ALWAYS ASK YOURSELF, 'CAN I BE THINKING BIGGER?'"

Kids of Immigrants

Immigrants are bold and persistent. They are dreamers and creative problem-solvers. Their innovative companies continue to shape our country.

Immigrants also impact America through their children. Kids of immigrants have built some of the world's most powerful companies. Simply put, America wouldn't be America without the following entrepreneurs!

Steve Jobs, son of a Syrian immigrant
• Cofounder of Apple
The late Steve Jobs was a visionary, a technology pioneer. He was also a once-in-a-generation entrepreneur. Steve was responsible for some of the world's most influential products, including the iPod, iPhone, and Macintosh computer. His company is worth over a trillion dollars!

Ruth Handler, daughter of Polish immigrants
• Cofounder of Mattel
Ruth Handler started Mattel with her husband, Elliot. The couple's most famous creation was the Barbie doll. Ruth was one of the first people to market toys to children instead of their parents. She advertised Barbie during *The Mickey Mouse Club*, a popular TV show for kids. Barbie became a huge success! Ruth and Elliot also created Hot Wheels, one of America's most popular toy cars.

Richard and Maurice "Mac" McDonald, sons of Irish immigrants
Ray Kroc, son of Czech immigrants
• Cofounders of McDonald's
In 1948, Richard and Mac were just two brothers with a hamburger restaurant. Their small company would become the largest burger chain in the world! The McDonald brothers were known for the efficient way they made food. A man named Ray Kroc took notice. Ray bought the McDonald's chain from Richard and Mac and turned their company into the ultra-successful franchise it is today.

Walt Disney, son of Canadian immigrants
• Founder of the Walt Disney Company
Walt Disney created a business unlike any in the world. His company manufactured magic. During his life, Walt brought the world Mickey Mouse, Donald Duck, Disneyland, and classic animated films. Today, Walt's company is just as magical—creating books, films, and experiences that shape popular culture.

Jeff Bezos, son of a Cuban immigrant
• Founder of Amazon
Amazon started as an online bookstore. It has become the world's most profitable web retailer. Jeff Bezos is the man behind the company's success. Since its founding in 1994, Amazon has become its own universe! It has acquired huge companies like Whole Foods and Twitch Interactive. Amazon also creates award-winning shows and films.

Estée Lauder, daughter of Czech and Hungarian immigrants
• Founder of Estée Lauder
Estée Lauder was the founder of the world-renowned company that shares her name. She created her fragrance, skin care, and cosmetics brand in 1946. Today, her products are popular all over the world. The Estée Lauder Companies are worth over $60 billion.

Koel Thomae

Australia

Cofounder of Noosa Yoghurt

After tasting a tub of homemade yogurt in the beachside town of Noosa, Australia, Koel Thomae saw a business opportunity. There was only one problem: She didn't know anything about yogurt.

Born in Australia, Koel was raised by a single mother who taught her the importance of responsibility and independence. By the time she was nine, Koel knew how to create a budget and manage her allowance money. These skills helped her to become a savvy businesswoman.

Koel moved to the United States and settled in Boulder, Colorado. There she worked at various food companies, including Izze, the makers of sparkling juices. On a trip to Australia to visit her family, she stopped by a farmers market where she tried a small tub of homemade local yogurt. Koel was blown away by the amazing flavor and creamy texture of this yogurt. It was sweet and tart at the same time. It was like nothing she had before, and nothing like the yogurts she had eaten in the United States.

The experience stayed with Koel, and two years later she flew back to Noosa to talk to the family that had made the yogurt. After a long lunch, the family agreed to let Koel use their recipe. Back in Colorado, Koel needed to find out how to turn this recipe into a company.

Koel didn't know anything about the dairy industry, and since milk is the main ingredient in yogurt, she needed to find a good partner. She found it in Rob Graves, the owner of a fourth-generation dairy farm in nearby Bellvue, Colorado. As soon as Rob tried Koel's yogurt he agreed to become her partner.

PERFECT PARTNERS

Koel knew she needed the right partner to launch Noosa. Rob Graves was an experienced dairy farmer. His commitment to producing high-quality, hormone-free milk lined up with Koel's goals. They became the perfect partners for the business.

The new partners had some connections in big stores like Whole Foods and Kroger. In 2012, Target decided to sell Noosa in more than 1,000 stores! Koel knew the tangy, full-fat yogurt that she loved a few years back in Australia was also loved in the United States.

The next few years were challenging for Koel and Rob. They never realized that Noosa would grow so quickly. Making enough yogurt to fulfill the demand put a lot of pressure on the partners. On top of that, Koel had a new baby girl, Matilda. She was busy.

"LIVE WITHIN YOUR MEANS AND INVEST IN EXPERIENCES OVER 'THINGS.'"

When Koel was 15 years old, she had gotten her first job in an ice-cream shop. The experience of working in the service industry taught her to be a good listener, see things across the entire company, and interact with many types of people. These skills came in handy when Koel and Rob needed to build a bigger plant and find the money to grow the company.

Today, Koel and Rob still own a big part of Noosa, but the business is co-owned by a big company. This has allowed Koel to do what she likes the most: develop new flavors using the best ingredients available, like salted caramel and blackberry serrano. She also works on Noosa Blooms for Bees, a program Koel created to support honeybees and Bee Friendly Farming. Koel's program has funded more than 20 BeeSmart® School Garden Kits for schools in Colorado so kids like you can learn all about honeybees.

BUSY BEES
Honey is an important ingredient in Noosa's yogurt, and in 2016 Koel and Rob decided to launch Noosa Blooms for Bees. The program supports honeybees and Bee Friendly Farming, which helps pollinators thrive in agricultural landscapes.

Carlos Castro

 *El Salvador*

Founder of Todos Supermarkets

Carlos Castro, born in 1955, grew up in Mejicanos, El Salvador. He shared a two-room home with his nine siblings and parents. The family had no running water. Carlos and his brothers and sisters worked from the time they were young.

In sixth grade, Carlos went to night school so that he could work during the day. He was a good student who loved learning about history and American culture. Carlos graduated from high school with honors and began studying business.

When civil war broke out in El Salvador in 1979, Carlos was 25. He knew it was time to leave the country. Carlos paid a smuggler $800 to illegally guide him across the US–Mexico border. But before long, he was caught and sent back to El Salvador.

"My dreams of being in the US or being safe were suddenly cut off," says Carlos. But he wasn't ready to give up. He crossed the border again and made it to California.

Carlos traveled to Washington, DC, and his wife, Gladis, soon joined him. Together, they were making their American dream come true. Carlos took whatever jobs he could get and did his best at them. "I was the best dishwasher in DC," he says.

While he worked hard at building a new life, Carlos also took classes in English and began the process of becoming a US citizen. He and Gladis bought a home, and after five years in America, they became citizens. Carlos felt incredibly proud: "I thought, this is a great opportunity."

Carlos had already started his own construction business but wanted to try something different. Looking around his neighborhood, Carlos realized that a grocery store could be a hub for immigrants. Housing was affordable, and it was close to the city. The neighborhood was already home to families from all over Central and Latin America.

In 1990, Carlos and Gladis decided "Todos" would be a great name for their grocery store. The name means "everyone." Todos specializes in Hispanic foods and groceries.

The store's success led the couple to open a second location. As they grew, their motto was "Identify the needs of the community." In addition to carrying groceries, they started offering services

"WE HAVE TO WORK HARD AND BELIEVE IN OURSELVES."

that the neighborhood needed. Todos has a barber shop inside one of its businesses, and a clothing store too. The grocery stores also offer tax assistance, money orders, and mail services.

Over time, people learned to come to Carlos and Gladis when they had questions. Carlos would talk to each person and help them however he could.

Today, Todos Supermarkets is worth more than $18 million. The supermarket chain employs over 150 people and is one of the biggest employers in Virginia's Prince William County. Carlos enjoys providing a trusted space for communities to gather. He often speaks to local youth about his story of success.

Carlos's message is simple: "If you have a good attitude and work hard, there is no limit to how high you can rise."

RESPECTFULLY YOURS
In his community, Carlos is called Don Carlos. "Don" is similar to "Sir." The word is used as a sign of respect.

Adi Tatarko & Alon Cohen

☆ *Israel*   ☆ *Israel*

Cofounders of Houzz

When Adi Tatarko met Alon Cohen on a bus in Thailand, starting a business was the last thing on her mind.

Adi was on vacation with friends. They were taking a 15-hour trip from Bangkok to the island of Ko Samui. By chance, the bus driver sat Adi next to Alon. The two chatted for the entire journey. "It was like four dates, one after another," Adi says. "It was wonderful."

Adi and Alon are both natives of Israel. When they returned to their home country, the couple dreamed of starting a software business. Two years after they met on the bus, Adi and Alon married.

Soon, the newlyweds moved to Silicon Valley in California. Exciting technology companies were everywhere. Alon went to work for eBay, and Adi found a job as a financial advisor.

The couple bought a house in Palo Alto that needed a lot of work. They also started a family. Between their demanding jobs and taking care of their children, Adi and Alon didn't have time to start their dream company.

The couple was frustrated by the home renovation process.

Having a hard time finding creative design ideas online, Adi and Alon cut pictures from magazines. They asked friends for referrals to trustworthy design contractors. At one point, the couple had to start the project over from scratch.

In the midst of the renovating chaos, Adi and Alon had a eureka moment. If there wasn't an online design resource for homeowners, they would make their own! The couple called their new project Houzz.

Adi comes from a long line of self-made women. Her grandmother was a fashion designer, and her mother worked in real estate. Adi knew how hard they had labored to be successful. She wasn't sure she wanted to do the same.

TEST MARKET
When Adi and Alon first started their business, they gave friends and neighbors a preview of Houzz. The couple also spoke with designers and architects. Both groups were excited about the company's concept. That's how Adi and Alon knew their idea would work!

Houzz started as a side project. The couple set up an office in their kitchen, and Alon coded the app at night after work. While Alon developed the website, Adi built an online community. "All of a sudden, I had more than a full-time job...but I really loved it," she says.

Houzz became a place for homeowners and professionals to connect. Designers and architects placed their portfolios on the website, where potential clients could find them. Homeowners also used the site for renovation inspiration. Houzz features interior design images from homes around the world.

Over the years, Adi and Alon have added many creative features to their site. Customers can use a 3D tool to imagine what new furniture will look like in a room or buy some of the pieces directly through the app.

Today, the company is worth over $4 billion. Adi is the CEO of Houzz, and Alon is its president. While the couple never dreamed Houzz would be a global hit, they are delighted to help people reinvent their homes!

"YOU CAN'T INNOVATE WITHOUT MAKING SOME MISTAKES ALONG THE WAY. THE KEY IS TO LEARN FROM THE FAILURE, AND TO TRY AGAIN."
—ADI TATARKO

Luis von Ahn

Guatemala

Founder of Duolingo

Over half of Guatemala's population lives in poverty. Most people cannot afford an education. Guatemalans who know English have a much greater chance of getting a good job. A native of the country, Luis von Ahn wants to help those in need. His company, Duolingo, aims to provide free language learning to everyone.

Luis was born in 1978. When he was a boy, his family owned a candy factory. Even then, Luis had a passion for technology. His curiosity for how things work led Luis to break candy machines just so he could put them back together! When he was eight, his parents bought him a computer, and Luis taught himself how to code.

In college, Luis wanted to study math. Unfortunately, there wasn't a school in Guatemala that offered a mathematics degree. Luis moved to the United States. He studied math at Duke University. Always eager to learn more, Luis was a diligent student.

At Carnegie Mellon University, Luis earned his PhD in computer science. After graduating, he became a professor at the college. Luis also began researching cryptography, a method that uses codes to keep information safe on computers.

Luis was just 21 when he came up with CAPTCHA. You may have seen CAPTCHA boxes online. They present distorted words that you have to type. The boxes help the website confirm that you are not a bot. They keep information safe. CAPTCHA stands for Completely Automated Public Turing test to tell Computers and Humans Apart.

After designing CAPTCHA, Luis became fascinated with the idea of "human computation." He was interested in how people and computers can work together to solve problems.

Luis joined forces with Severin Hacker, a student interested in the same ideas. Both men were eager to help the millions of people around the world who needed to learn English. The tech duo knew that online language courses were expensive.

Luis and Severin designed a free language-learning app. They called it Duolingo. The app looks and feels like a game. You can use it on your own or learn a new language with others.

When Luis and Severin developed Duolingo, they thought the app would be helpful for translation as well as language learning. Their program would serve two purposes.

SPEAKING IN DIFFERENT TONGUES

According to an independent study, spending 34 hours on Duolingo is like taking a college-level language course. Depending on how hard a language is to learn, experts say it takes between 480 and 720 hours to learn a new language.

"THE OPPORTUNITIES FOR IMPACT ARE REAL AND HAVE THE POTENTIAL TO MATTER TO SO MANY PEOPLE."

First, it would teach learners for free. Second, it would rely on users to translate other texts. But after three years, the two men dropped the translation side of their business. They decided to focus Duolingo solely on language learning.

The program is a unique tool because its lessons are created by volunteers all over the world. More than 300 people teach their native languages on the app.

According to Luis, "Somebody who doesn't have a bank account should be able to use all of the learning content of Duolingo. That's our stated goal and we remain true to it to this day."

Duolingo has more than 30 million users. The app offers instruction in 30 different languages, with more languages to come.

The program is also partnering with schools in Colombia to help students learn English. Luis estimates that 20% of language classrooms in the United States use the app.

SPEAK YOUR (FAVORITE) LANGUAGE
Most people use Duolingo to learn English, Spanish, or French. But you can also use the app to learn Klingon if you're a *Star Trek* fan, or Valyrian if you like *Game of Thrones.*

BY THE NUMBERS
3 minutes: the length of a Duolingo lesson

30 million: the number of active Duolingo users

300 million: the number of registered users worldwide

$700 million: Duolingo's net worth

Luis's driving passion is making a difference. "If we increased the number of people that were able to learn English by five or ten percent in the world, that would be amazing."

Sophia Grojsman

Belarus

Perfumer

Even as a girl, Sophia Grojsman was known for her keen sense of smell. One of her favorite childhood games was identifying flowers by their scent! Sophia loved the outdoors. Unlike other children, she didn't care about playing with toys. Flowers, birds, and trees—these were the things she adored.

Sophia's mother used her daughter's special talent for practical purposes. At the market, she would ask Sophia to smell the milk, butter, and cheese. If the little girl made a face, her mother knew the food was not fresh.

Sophia was born in 1945 in Belarus. When she was 15, Sophia moved with her family to Poland. Focusing her studies on chemistry, she earned a degree in science. Just a few years later, the family moved again—this time to New York. They had been invited by a Jewish family that Sophia's father had saved during World War II. He had been a part of the Russian resistance. Sophia says, "He helped save a group of Jewish people, including my mother, who were hiding from the Nazis."

The family settled in Brooklyn. She looked for work through the Hebrew Immigrant Aid Society (HIAS). The society is a safe haven for immigrants and refugees. It has helped people find food, shelter, jobs, and transportation. Through HIAS, Sophia found her dream job. She was hired by International Flavors & Fragrances (IFF).

At her new job, Sophia was trained in the art of perfumery. Her teachers were Ernest Shiftan and Josephine Catapano. They were both master perfumers. With their training, Sophia soon learned that "fragrance chemistry" was very different from the chemistry she had studied in college. However, Sophia says, "I was very curious, and this quality helped me learn quickly."

Sophia's superiors took notice of her talent. "When IFF realized I understood fragrance, not just the mixing, but the logic—I'm logical, and I was always good in math—they liked me."

She began creating her own perfumes. From the beginning, Sophia was an innovator! She discovered a new way to design fragrances. Her perfumes were simple, made up of just four to seven ingredients. For Sophia, making perfume was like making music. Each scent was a "note," and all of the notes had to blend together to create a beautiful harmony.

Over the past several decades, Sophia has invented some of the world's most popular and memorable fragrances. These include perfumes like Eternity, Paris, and

KNEES, PLEASE
Most people dab perfume on their wrists or on their necks. But Sophia says the best place to put perfume is on the back of your knees! "Fragrance rises," she says. When you spray perfume behind your knees, the scent will surround you.

Trésor. At one point, Sophia says, Trésor was more popular than the world's most famous perfume, Chanel N°5.

Sophia's most successful perfumes all have one thing in common: flowers. Since she was a child, Sophia has loved roses, jasmine, and violets. The rose remains her favorite scent. "Rose is a flower of love," she says.

SMELLS LIKE SUCCESS
Sophia has created world famous perfumes, including:
- White Linen, Estée Lauder (1978)
- Paris, Yves Saint Laurent (1983)
- Eternity, Calvin Klein (1988)
- Trésor, Lancôme (1990)
- Magic, Celine (1996)

Sophia has lived in America for many decades and is thankful for the opportunities the country has provided. Still, she remains a Belarusian at heart. "Despite all of the changes in my life, the roots will remain, and one cannot forget the soil upon which one grew up. You can take me out of Russia, but you cannot take Russia out of me."

"IN A STRANGE WAY, IT'S LIKE CRAFTING MUSIC, BUT THIS IS CREATING SMELL. PERFUME IS MUSIC FOR PEOPLE'S SOULS."

Pierre Omidyar

▌▌ *France*

Founder of eBay

Pierre Omidyar might be a multibillionaire, but he isn't your typical rich guy. He doesn't spend time shopping for expensive cars or buying mansions. Instead, Pierre wants to invest in people. He helps others launch companies that make the world a better place.

Born in Paris in 1967 to Iranian parents, Pierre moved with his family to Maryland when he was child. His father had accepted a residency at the famous Johns Hopkins University Medical Center.

In high school, Pierre was more interested in working with computers than attending classes. He often snuck away from gym class to spend time in the computer lab. Instead of sending Pierre to detention, his principal asked him to write a program. Using his new skills, Pierre did just that. He designed a program that printed library catalog cards.

Pierre went on to study computer science at Tufts University. After graduating, he worked for several software companies as an engineer. Pierre even set up his own business with friends called eShop. The computer software company caught Microsoft's attention. Microsoft's purchase of eShop was Pierre's first major business success!

While working as an engineer, Pierre's hobbies were designing web pages and writing code. In 1995, he started toying with the

> "EVERYTHING I'VE DONE IS ROOTED IN THE NOTION THAT EVERY HUMAN BEING IS BORN EQUALLY CAPABLE. WHAT PEOPLE LACK IS EQUAL OPPORTUNITY. MY GOAL HAS BEEN TO EXPAND OPPORTUNITY TO AS MANY PEOPLE AS POSSIBLE SO THEY CAN REACH THEIR POTENTIAL."

idea of an auction website where people could buy and sell things.

Pierre started designing an online marketplace. This was the beginning of eBay! When it came time to test the site, Pierre listed a broken laser pointer for sale. He started the bidding at $1. After a week, bidding had pushed the price of the laser to $15. Pierre reached out to be sure the buyer knew the pointer didn't work. The buyer knew—he couldn't afford to buy a working laser pointer. He planned to fix it!

PEZ, PLEASE

Long ago, Pierre's girlfriend Pam was obsessed with Pez candy dispensers. She collected them, often hunting for them online. Pierre created eBay so that his girlfriend could easily connect with other collectors. If it weren't for Pez, eBay might not exist! Pam and Pierre were later married.

At first, Pierre didn't make any money from the auctions. But he watched as people flooded onto eBay. Within a few months, he moved the site to a bigger platform. People were buying, selling, and trading all kinds of stuff! Collectors flocked to eBay to talk to other people with similar interests.

Pierre realized it wasn't just about

buying and selling. It was about social connection. Most people on the site treated each other with respect, even though they were strangers. "This was something that was new for folks—this sense of values," Pierre explains. "If you can get over this initial distrust that people have of strangers, you can do remarkable things."

Growing rapidly, eBay went public in 1998. Pierre became an overnight billionaire. Right away, he and his wife, Pam, decided to give back. "I had the notion that, ok, so now we have all of this wealth, we could buy not only one expensive car, we could buy all of them," says Pierre. "As soon as you realize that you could buy all of them, then none of them are particularly interesting or satisfying."

I GOT IT ON EBAY
One of the most expensive items ever sold on eBay was a 405-foot super yacht. An anonymous buyer bought the boat for a cool $170 million. The giant yacht has a movie theater, 8 guest cabins, a gym, and even a place to park a helicopter.

They founded the Omidyar Foundation, which supports other people's great ideas. The foundation has invested more than a billion dollars in companies that are tackling global problems. Pierre's lifetime goal is to give away most of his wealth.

Francesca & Elena Cavallo Favilli

■ ■ *Italy*　　　　　■ ■ *Italy*

Cofounders of Timbuktu Labs

Francesca Cavallo and Elena Favilli know the power of telling a good story. The story they told together sparked a worldwide wave of inspiration.

Francesca and Elena met in Italy, where they both grew up. The women were born just a year apart. Francesca, a playwright and director, was born in 1983. Elena, a journalist, was born in 1982.

The couple fell in love and started a company together. Timbuktu Labs focused on combining technology with learning. Their first project was creating a kids magazine formatted for the iPad. The project was a success! The two women decided to leave Italy and move to California to continue pursuing their dreams.

Francesca and Elena moved to Silicon Valley, the land of startups. "We were always the only women in the room. We kept hearing that two girls alone will never raise serious capital."

In 2015, Elena wrote an article about how it felt to be a woman in Silicon Valley. Even though everyone was focused on the future, it felt like they were stuck in the past. She said that how women were treated was practically prehistoric. It felt like only men were taken seriously.

> "IT IS IMPORTANT TO CULTIVATE, ESPECIALLY IF YOU ARE A WOMAN OR A GIRL, A REBEL ATTITUDE, A REBEL CHARACTER BECAUSE YOU HAVE TO FIGHT HARDER TO REACH YOUR DREAM AND TO GET WHAT YOU WANT."

Francesca and Elena were frustrated. They had great ideas they wanted to share but couldn't get the funding to move forward. They moved to Los Angeles, taking their best idea with them.

FACT-FINDING

Before they created the book, Elena and Francesca did their research to show funders why a book like theirs was needed. They consulted two research studies and found that in children's shows, only 18% of the female characters have a job or show ambition, while 80% of male characters do. That's a big difference!

Elena and Francesca were inspired to create a different kind of fairy tale for girls. They thought of the title first: *Good Night Stories for Rebel Girls*. The idea was to show young girls that anything was possible.

They created a book full of inspiring stories about 100 great women. These included women from the past and from today, from Queen Elizabeth I to Serena Williams. Francesca and Elena chose women from all over the world. They wrote about artists and athletes, scientists and authors. Each woman's story was paired with an illustration by a female artist too.

Instead of relying on getting funding the traditional way, Francesca and Elena decided to turn to the internet. They started a Kickstarter campaign. The goal was to raise $40,000 for the first printing. Not only did they make their goal, they made history! They broke the record for crowdfunding for a children's book.

Francesca and Elena raised almost $700,000. Then, they raised another $900,000! Altogether, 25,000 people from 75 countries around the world pitched in to help fund the book.

Rebel Girls was a smash hit. Francesca and Elena received comments and notes from girls all over the world. Some readers suggested other women they admired.

FAST FACTS: ITALY
Official Name: Italian Republic
Capital: Rome
Population: 60.34 million
Official Language: Italian
Currency: Euro
Area: 116,631 square miles

REBEL SPIRIT
Goodnight Stories for Rebel Girls stayed in the top ten on the *New York Times* best-seller list for 42 weeks. There is also a podcast and an audio version of the book. In the Women's March of January 2017, protestors held signs inspired by the book. "We are proud that our book has become a symbol of resistance," says Francesca.

It inspired them to create another book, *Good Night Stories for Rebel Girls 2*. They raised more than enough crowd funds for that book too. Altogether, Elena and Francesca have sold more than 2.5 million books all over the world.

In an interview shortly after their first book came out, they said, "There isn't just one way to be a rebel, there are many different ways and you just have to find yours."

Pioneering Entrepreneurs

1806

William Colgate, an immigrant from England, starts a soap and candle business in New York City. His company later sells the first tubed toothpaste!

1837

English immigrant William Procter and Irish immigrant James Gamble found Procter & Gamble. Today, the company makes many popular household products.

1869

Marcus Goldman, a German immigrant, founds Goldman Sachs. The company becomes a globally successful investment bank.

1892

General Electric is founded, thanks in large part to Elihu Thomson, an English immigrant and electrical engineer. Elihu has been called a "founder of the US electrical industry."

Most of the companies featured in this book are new. They were founded within the last few decades. But there are immigrant-founded businesses that have been around for much longer. These companies have grown alongside our country. The people who started them were pioneers!

1915
William Fox, a Hungarian immigrant, founds the Fox Film Corporation.

1939
Nathan Cummings, a Canadian immigrant, acquires a company that will become the Sara Lee Corporation. The business produces frozen and fresh foods as well as household products.

1901
Swedish immigrant John W. Nordstrom opens Wallin & Nordstrom, a shoe store. Today, Nordstrom is an incredibly successful fashion retailer that sells everything from clothing and shoes to home goods!

1903
Canadian immigrant James L. Kraft starts a business delivering cheese. His company would grow to become Kraft Foods. Kraft cheese, Planters nuts, and Jell-O desserts are all produced by Kraft Foods.

Tae Yun Kim
 *South Korea*

Founder of Jung SuWon Martial Arts Academy and Lighthouse Worldwide Solutions

What if your earliest memory was being told that you were a curse? Tae Yun Kim was born in 1946 in a tiny South Korean village. Her parents were hoping for a baby boy. When Tae Yun was born, her family called her curse. Her mother, ashamed of not having a son, often left the little girl without food. The other children in the village made fun of Tae Yun, calling her a curse too.

When Tae Yun was five years old, the Korean War raged in her village. In the chaos, Tae Yun was abandoned by her family. Bombs fell around the young girl as she fled the village. Somehow, she was spared.

Tae Yun knew then that she wasn't a curse! If she was curse, how had she survived the bombing?

After the war, Tae Yun went to live with her grandparents. At her new home, Tae Yun's uncles practiced tae kwon do. The traditional Korean martial art is more than a way of fighting—it is a way to unite the mind and body.

Tae Yun was fascinated. She begged her uncles to teach her, but they refused. It was forbidden to teach tae kwon do to girls. Tae Yun's uncles told her to focus on learning to cook and sew. They wanted her to be ready to have a family of her own.

Tae Yun didn't want to learn how to cook and sew—she wanted to learn tae kwon do! Tae Yun continued to pester her family. When she was seven, she finally convinced one of her uncles. He agreed, thinking the girl would give up right away.

FAST FACTS: SOUTH KOREA
Official Name: Republic of Korea
Capital: Seoul
Population: 52 million
Official Language: Korean
Currency: Won
Area: 37,491 square miles

Tae Yun never gave up on tae kwon do. She trained hard and eventually met a Buddhist master who became her new teacher. The master suggested that Tae Yun and her family move to America.

No one in Tae Yun's family spoke English. When the family landed in Burlington, Vermont, they had just $300 to start their new life.

Tae Yun was eager to share what she had learned about martial arts. She dreamed of opening a tae kwon do school but had trouble finding someone who would rent her the space. To make a living, Tae Yun worked three jobs: pumping gas, cleaning a local hotel, and selling cars.

Over the next ten years, Tae Yun began teaching and developing her own form of tae kwon do, called Jung SuWon. It is a gentler form of the martial art—less about competition and more about connecting mind, body, and spirit.

"IF I CAN ACHIEVE MY GOALS IN THIS LIFETIME, OTHERS CAN DO THE SAME—NEVER GIVE UP!"

GOING FOR GOLD

Tae kwon do is an ancient practice. It is more than 2,000 years old and is related to karate and kung fu. Tae kwon do first appeared in the Olympics in the Summer Games of 1988 in Seoul. The martial art is the official national sport of South Korea.

After years of practice, Tae Yun became one of the highest-ranking female martial artists in the world. She was a tae kwon do grandmaster! In 1978, Tae Yun coached the US women's tae kwon do team at the Pre-World Games. Her team won a gold medal!

While building her tae kwon do school, Tae Yun was also designing a very different kind of business. She created Lighthouse Worldwide Solutions to have an even greater impact on the world. Lighthouse systems monitor contamination to ensure that ultra-clean environments stay clean.

As a businesswoman, Tae Yun has received multiple awards for her successes. The little girl who was once called a curse was even named "The Hope of the Country of Korea" by the president of South Korea.

MIND OVER MATTER

Tae Yun's students call her Great Grandmaster Kim. Her motto is, "He Can Do, She Can Do, Why Not Me!" She has performed many amazing martial arts feats, including walking on fire and laying on a bed of nails. Tae Yun's YouTube channel features many of her awe-inspiring feats.

"I teach how to put your body and mind together, to recognize your strengths and weaknesses, and rise above them," says Tae Yun.

Tae Yun Kim persevered through many difficulties and has inspired others to pursue their dreams, no matter how challenging the path may be.

Laura Behrens Wu

■ *Germany*

Cofounder and CEO of Shippo

Growing up as the daughter of a German diplomat, Laura Behrens Wu had a unique upbringing. Her family moved around a lot. Laura was born in Germany and lived in China and Ecuador as a child.

"Seeing poverty...at a young age, made me realize how privileged my life had been so far," says Laura. "It made me want to make the most out of it."

Laura's family moved to the United States when she was a young girl. She was a motivated student and an early entrepreneur. During college, Laura sold handbags online to earn extra cash. Business was good, but there was one problem: the shipping.

Shipping was troublesome for a few reasons. First, it took up a lot of time and energy. Laura spent hours going to the post office, waiting in line, and calculating shipping costs. Second, it was very expensive to ship internationally.

Laura was losing business because of high shipping costs. Customers were used to getting fast and free shipping from big online retailers like Amazon. After doing some research, she discovered that customers were canceling their orders. They would see the shipping cost and decide not to buy products as a result. Laura knew there had to be a better way for small businesses to ship their merchandise.

Retailers like Amazon work with many different shipping providers. It's easy for them to shop around and find cheap shipping. Small businesses don't have that kind of power. They don't have as many connections as large retailers.

Laura's vision was to create a powerful resource that made shipping easier and more affordable for small businesses. Together, with cofounder Simon Kreuz, that's exactly what she did.

BORING BIZ?

If you think shipping sounds like a boring industry, you're not alone. At first, Laura and Simon weren't sure about starting a shipping company. But after they did some research, the two entrepreneurs realized that there were tons of ways they could improve shipping. The idea of revolutionizing an industry got Laura and Simon excited to start Shippo.

"We power shipping for businesses," Laura says. Shippo helps find the best shipping rates. The company also helps businesses with buying shipping labels, tracking packages, and returning packages.

As Laura was building her business, she learned the power of determination. She and Simon pitched their idea to 125 investors. Over a hundred of the investors said no.

CANINE CORPORATION

If you look on Shippo's website, you'll find portraits of the company's employees. Among them: Bruce the Cultural Advisor, Brady the Cleaner, and Jack the Greeter. These valued employees have four legs instead of two. They're Shippo's canine staff! Paws up for Bruce, Brady, and Jack.

> "THERE IS NO SINGLE WAY HOW A GREAT FOUNDER SHOULD [LOOK]. THERE IS NO OVERNIGHT SUCCESS. IT'S A LOT ABOUT HARD WORK. IT'S ABOUT BEING PERSISTENT. IT'S ABOUT STANDING UP AGAIN AFTER YOU FALL."

Laura and Simon succeeded because they refused to give up. They worked hard to prove that Shippo was a service that customers needed and wanted. "We used each opportunity to get better and improve," Laura says. "The first dozen pitches were terrible. The next several dozen gave us room to practice."

Eventually, the cofounders were able to raise the money they needed to launch the company. Since then, Shippo has helped more than 35,000 online businesses ship their products. Laura's company has transported more than $5 billion worth of merchandise!

After living all over the world, Laura thinks the United States was the best place to start her business. "The raw amount of talent and people to talk to, to bounce ideas off is unmatched anywhere else," she says. "They don't look at your age or your experience. They look at how hard you work and your execution."

IT'S IN THE MAIL
Shippo has helped many small businesses ship their goods. The company has shipped everything from custom wedding dresses and miniature building materials to eyeglasses and underwear. Shippo assists with over 100 million shipments each year.

Frank Gehry

I+I *Canada*

Architect

As a boy growing up in Toronto, Canada, Frank Gehry loved
building things. Enchanted by the unusual objects in his
grandfather's hardware store, Frank often built tiny cities out of
the curious items he found there.

Frank was born in 1929. When he was a teen, his family moved to Los
Angeles—they didn't have much. Frank, just 17, worked as a truck
driver during the day. At night, he studied at Los Angeles City
College. There, he fell in love with architecture.

As soon as he was able, Frank went to the University of Southern
California. He studied architectural design. Frank's studies were
interrupted when he was drafted into the army. But as soon as his
service was done, Frank returned to design. This time, he attended
Harvard University.

Frank wasn't satisfied at Harvard. He decided to return to Los
Angeles. Back in the city he loved, Frank started building houses.
Pooling savings with a friend, he bought a plot of land for a six-unit
apartment complex. It was the beginning of his firm, Frank Gehry
and Associates.

The first project to bring him recognition was his family home
in Santa Monica. Using chain link, plywood, and corrugated, or
ridged, metal, Frank's design looked more like a sculpture than a

house. Some people loved the design, and others didn't. Either way, people started recognizing Frank's work.

It wasn't long before Frank was creating buildings all around the world. In the 1990s, Frank designed Seattle's Museum of Pop Culture. Some say the building looks like a giant metal skirt, flapping in the wind. Others say the building looks like a smashed electric guitar!

Frank also designed the Dancing House in Prague. The building is often called "Fred and Ginger." Its two main towers look like they are dancing with each other, just like old Hollywood entertainers Fred Astaire and Ginger Rogers.

Frank has designed skyscrapers, museums, music halls, and outdoor spaces, like the Jay Pritzker Pavilion at Millennium Park in Chicago.

THAT'S A GEHRY!
Frank's buildings are instantly recognizable. His unique sense of design combines creative angles with unusual materials.

"I TEST IDEAS ENDLESSLY AND ASK WHY... YOU DON'T JUST DO THE FIRST IDEA THAT COMES TO YOU, WHICH IS EASY. IT'S NOT FAIR TO DO ANYTHING LESS THAN YOUR BEST."

WIND IN THE SAILS

Frank's design for the Walt Disney Concert Hall in Los Angeles was inspired by one of his favorite hobbies: sailing. The building's metal sheets look like they are waving in the wind. The iconic building is a hallmark of the city.

Each of Frank's works is a masterpiece. His creations are original and surprising, often bringing a sense of joy and awe to those who see them.

Over the years, Frank has won many awards. The most notable is the Pritzker Architecture Prize. It is a lifetime achievement award. The Pritzker is only given to designers who have made "significant contributions to humanity." In 2016, Frank received the Presidential Medal of Freedom from President Barack Obama. This award is the highest honor given to civilians who are pioneers in areas including the arts, science, and human rights.

Frank has often been inspired by the work of other artists. When he was young, Frank visited Greece and saw an inspiring statue. He says, "Fifty years ago, I visited Delphi and saw that statue. The label said 'artist unknown.' It made me cry, that someone could make something... that could move someone thousands of years later."

From a little boy building cardboard cities to an award-winning designer, Frank Gehry has certainly moved us with his dazzling designs.

CARDBOARD CREATIVITY

Before he became a famous architect, Frank designed unusual furniture. Made between 1969 and 1973, his Easy Edges furniture series was made almost completely out of cardboard.

Ishveen Anand

🇬🇧 *England and* 🇮🇳 *India*

Founder of OpenSponsorship

Ishveen Anand has always played to win. Growing up, she was a star athlete in cricket and netball. She was even named captain of the cricket and netball teams at Oxford University.

Sports and winning remain important to Ishveen. As an entrepreneur, she is determined to succeed, no matter the odds. Today, Ishveen works in the world of professional sports, an industry filled with men.

"When I go into a room, I have to work 20 times harder for you to trust that I am an expert in this industry," she says.

As a British woman of Indian descent, working in sports has never been easy. "Being a girl in the sports world makes it easier to get noticed and remembered," Ishveen says. "But it's harder to be taken serious at the senior level. People always thought I was my client's daughter!"

Ishveen's passion for sports led her to a job at an Indian sports management agency. She moved to Delhi, India, to pursue her dreams. As a sports agent, Ishveen sold rights for athletic teams.

After gaining experience in the field, she decided to start her own company. She wanted to help Indian athletes attract sponsors from other countries. But not long after starting her company, she got married. Her husband's business moved them to New York.

Keeping the sponsorship business she started in India afloat while living in New York was very difficult for Ishveen. She had to let her company go. Luckily, she soon had an exciting idea for a new business.

Living in New York had inspired Ishveen's latest business idea. She noticed that city life was totally reliant on technology. Whether Ishveen was getting a taxi or ordering food, she did it online. But in the world of sports agents, nothing was digital. Everyone relied on connecting in person or over the phone.

That's how Ishveen's company, OpenSponsorship, was born. She wanted to create a digital space for athletes and brands to connect. Ishveen knew it would work. Many industries were thriving online. Through the internet, people were dating, finding jobs, buying houses, and meeting new friends.

THE MORE, THE MERRIER!
OpenSponsorship is attracting more and more people. There are thousands of athletes and brands on the site. Deals between athletes and brands have surpassed $1.6 million. It's a powerful place to connect!

OpenSponsorship is an online marketplace where athletes and brands can find each other. Companies pay a small fee to join and get access to profiles of thousands of athletes, from superstars to those who are just making a name for themselves.

Brands hire athletes for different reasons. One company may be looking for an athlete to promote its shampoo. Another may need an athlete to appear at a special event. How can these brands tell who will be a good fit?

Ishveen's website shows companies data on each athlete. This data includes social media stats. Once a company finds a good fit, it makes the athlete an offer. The athlete receives the offer quickly, sometimes within 24 hours.

Both athletes and brands liked the site. OpenSponsorship was a success! Ishveen was called a digital trailblazer.

Ishveen's plans for the future are big. She believes sponsorships will go global, crossing more borders as different sports become popular in other countries. Ishveen hopes OpenSponsorship will be the way athletes and brands connect, no matter where they are in the world.

"THE BEST WAY TO GET THINGS DONE IS TO GET INVOLVED. DELEGATION IS GREAT, BUT AT SOME POINT IF YOU CAN SHOW YOUR TEAM THAT YOU ARE READY TO DO THAT SAME WORK, IT CAN LEAD TO GREAT THINGS."

Claudia & Azam Mirza Mirza

■ Colombia　■ India

Cofounders of Akorbi

When Claudia Mirza was just four years old, her father moved to the United States. Claudia and her mother were left behind in one of the poorest areas of Medellin, Colombia. The young girl often wondered if she would see her father again. Struggling to make ends meet, Claudia and her mother relied on the kindness of friends and strangers.

"It took a lot of creativity for my mother and I to really make it," she says. "We just had a bag with clothes. I remember going from house to house with our bag, asking people to let us live in their homes."

Despite her hardships, Claudia was an excellent student. She studied hard and won a scholarship to a local private school. When she was almost done with high school, Claudia's father asked her to join him in America. She begged him to take her mother instead.

Claudia stayed in Colombia and went to a technical college. Then, many years after her father had left, Claudia was reunited with her parents in the United States.

She went right to work, getting a job at a large telecommunications company. Claudia also went back to school to earn a degree in business. Soon, she met her future husband. Azam Mirza was a smart

> ## "I HAVE NEVER STOPPED WORKING HARD A DAY IN MY LIFE TO ACHIEVE MY GOALS."
> —CLAUDIA MIRZA

young engineer and an immigrant from India. After Claudia and Azam were married, the couple settled in Texas. It seemed like their dreams of success in America were coming true. But in 2002, there was a dot-com crash. Claudia lost her job.

The young couple had to change their plans. While they were figuring out their next steps, Claudia helped her father at his job: training horses at a racetrack.

One day, during an important workshop at the racetrack, the interpreter who was supposed to help translate the training didn't show up. The organizers looked frantically for someone to fill in.

GOING GLOBAL
Akorbi provides services in more than 170 different languages. The company's staff helps with telephone calls, emails, and chats. Akorbi representatives are located all over the world, in the United States, Latin America, and Africa.

Claudia stepped in! She enjoyed translating the workshop into Spanish. She realized translating was a perfect job for her. Claudia and Azam decided to start their own business. "I started a business to survive," says Claudia. The company was called Akorbi.

"I had the creative idea and Azam is great at operations and is amazing at numbers," Claudia says. "We made a great team."

Akorbi started out as a translation service. The need for quality translation was shared by many industries. Soon, Akorbi was getting jobs from huge companies. They were even hired by the US government!

Today, the company has more than 900 employees. Akorbi's annual revenue is close to $55 million.

Claudia and Azam think giving back is important. They are committed to helping others achieve their dreams. Claudia is especially excited to help her home country.

FROM COAST TO COAST

Colombia is the only South American country that has beaches on both the Pacific Ocean and the Caribbean Sea. Colombia is also known for its coffee and its talented musicians. Both Shakira and Juanes were born in Colombia.

"It has taken me a lifetime to achieve dreams," says Claudia. "But I like to finish things. There is something that I would like to finish...I would like to go back to Colombia and help women and little girls that have a dream to succeed. I want to empower them to be self-sufficient and believe in themselves and launch their businesses so they help generations."

AWARD-WINNING GROWTH

Akorbi has grown over 200% in recent years. In 2015, Azam and Claudia received the Immigrant Entrepreneur Award. In 2018, Akorbi was named one of the fastest-growing woman-owned businesses in the world.

José Andrés

 *Spain*

Founder of World Central Kitchen

José Andrés is a world-famous chef. He is best known for helping make Spanish food popular in the United States. But José's legacy goes far beyond the *tapas* he has joyfully served to hungry Americans.

José was born in 1969 in Asturias, Spain, and grew up outside of Barcelona. He left school at 14 but later returned to study cooking. After serving in the Spanish navy, José worked as a professional cook. Then, he moved to New York City to work at a restaurant with a friend.

José worked hard and built a reputation as an exceptional chef. In 1993, he opened his first restaurant. The young chef would open dozens more in the years to come.

José has won cooking awards, written bestselling cookbooks, and been featured on many television shows. But his real claim to fame is founding World Central Kitchen, a nonprofit organization that provides food to people who have been affected by natural disasters.

In 2010, a massive earthquake hit Haiti. José wanted to help. He went to Haiti and saw the earthquake's devastating effects. There were many people struggling to survive. They did not have access to food or water. José knew he had to do something; he created World Central Kitchen.

José's foundation educates professional chefs all over the world. It teaches food safety and even builds kitchens. After Haiti, the foundation helped people in need in Cambodia, Peru, and Brazil.

In 2017, when Hurricane Harvey landed in Houston, José traveled to Texas to see what he could do. He helped local chefs serve thousands of meals to those affected by the hurricane.

Later that year, Hurricane Maria hit the island of Puerto Rico. The storm was devastating. Relief from the US government wasn't getting to Puerto Ricans fast enough. José knew he had to find a way to get food to the people.

HAM AND CHEESE, PLEASE

José's signature ham and cheese sandwich is an easy meal to prepare and transport. When Hurricane Dorian struck the Bahamas in 2019, Word Central Kitchen worked together with stranded resort guests to put together thousands of sandwiches.

Within a few days, José and his team arrived on the island. They brought 250,000 pounds of food with them. The team connected with other chefs and found working kitchens they could use.

World Central Kitchen became the island's primary source of food. As the island waited for power to return, José and his team kept cooking. On the busiest days, they were cooking and serving about 175,000 meals. All together, World Central Kitchen served over 3.6 million meals!

It's really important to remember that José is a restaurant chef. He has not been specially trained to cook for thousands during a natural disaster. But José's lack of experience hasn't stopped him from doing what is needed. World Central Kitchen has served more than 10 million meals during 24 disasters.

Many people have helped José bring meals to people in need. More than 44,000 volunteers have supported World Central Kitchen and its mission.

José's greatest hope is that each person will see themselves in those who are struggling. He says, "I am my wife, I am my daughters, I am my cooks, I am my chefs, I am my community. I think everybody should be saying 'I am them.'"

During the COVID-19 pandemic, José and his World Central Kitchen team provided over 160,000 fresh meals a day to communities in need, fulfilling his dream of "a world where there is always a warm meal, an encouraging word, and a helping hand in hard times."

What Kind of Entrepreneur Are You?

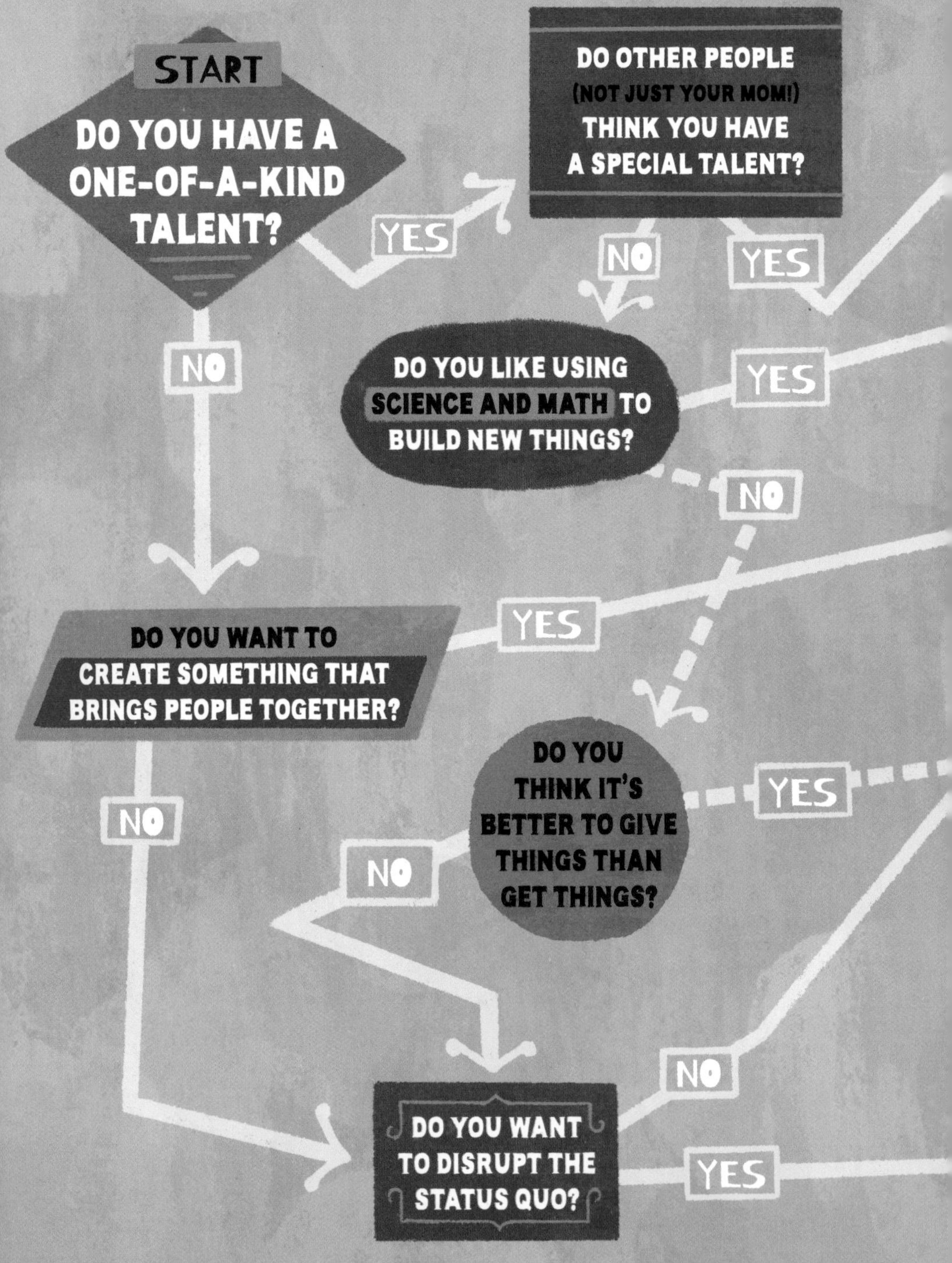

START

DO YOU HAVE A ONE-OF-A-KIND TALENT?

YES

NO

DO OTHER PEOPLE (NOT JUST YOUR MOM!) THINK YOU HAVE A SPECIAL TALENT?

NO

YES

YES

DO YOU LIKE USING SCIENCE AND MATH TO BUILD NEW THINGS?

NO

YES

DO YOU WANT TO CREATE SOMETHING THAT BRINGS PEOPLE TOGETHER?

NO

YES

DO YOU THINK IT'S BETTER TO GIVE THINGS THAN GET THINGS?

YES

NO

NO

DO YOU WANT TO DISRUPT THE STATUS QUO?

NO

YES

DO YOU CONSIDER YOURSELF AN ARTIST?

YES

NO

DO YOU WANT TO DESIGN AND BUILD A TOTALLY NEW PRODUCT?

YES

NO

NO

YES

DO YOU THINK THE BEST WAY TO SPEND MONEY IS TO GIVE IT AWAY?

CREATOR
You are a creator at heart. You have a unique talent that you want to share with the world. You might be a writer, musician, or perfumer (see Sophia Grojsman). Whatever business you start should grow out of your talent.

INVENTOR
You were the kid who loved Legos. Maybe you still do! Building things is your happy place. Like Ayah Bdeir, you want to invent something totally new.

CONNECTOR
You love introducing friends to each other. You want to build a business that connects people. Whether it's online or IRL, your business will provide a new way for people to interact.

GIVER
More than anything you want to help others. If your business is successful you will delight in sharing your wealth. Like Daniel Lubetzky, kindness is what drives you to create!

DISRUPTER
You go against the grain. Like Laura Behrens Wu, you aren't satisfied with the status quo. If something isn't working, you will find a new solution. Laura is changing the shipping industry. What industry will you change?

Conclusion

The very first immigrants to this country were the Native Americans who walked over a land bridge that connected Asia to North America during the last Ice Age.

Over the 20,000 years since then, immigrants from all over the world have made America their home.

Throughout the centuries, people have immigrated to this country seeking freedom, fortune, and independence. Their reasons for coming are as varied as the places they came from.

At times in our history, immigrants were welcomed to America. Their differences and their cultures were celebrated.

At other times, Americans didn't want to welcome them. They were worried about disease and crime. Sometimes, immigrants have been blamed for taking too much or bringing unwanted change.

But as we have learned through the success stories in this book, those who come can be powerful change makers too.

Some people move to the United States for a better education or because their business brings them here. Others come because of safety, family, or love.

The stories in this book show that immigrants are part of the fabric of America. Their successes are our successes. When they do well, we do well.

Their determination to prosper and create a better life makes life better for us all.

The people featured in this book have incredible ambition. Maybe it's because many of them struggled so hard to get here.

Their ideas have made our lives better. Some used their creativity, by cooking wonderful food or designing beautiful things. Others took simple ideas and made them better, from smarter shipping to healthier nutrition bars.

And some helped us better connect with each other. They made online communities or volunteered in ways that changed the world.

The stories in this book are big success stories. But for every big dream come true, there are thousands of small dreams that come true too. We are surrounded by stories of successful immigrants, no matter where we live in America.

Maybe you know someone who is the first in their family to move to the United States. Maybe you know someone else whose parents were the first to come.

All Americans have ancestors who came from somewhere other than America. Without them, we wouldn't be here today.

One of America's greatest symbols of freedom is the Statue of Liberty. She stands on Liberty Island, just off the coast of New York. More than 300 feet tall, the statue holds a torch to light the way of those coming to the shores of America.

On her tablet, it reads:

GIVE ME YOUR TIRED, YOUR POOR,
YOUR HUDDLED MASSES YEARNING TO BREATHE FREE,
THE WRETCHED REFUSE OF YOUR TEEMING SHORE.
SEND THESE, THE HOMELESS, TEMPEST-TOST TO ME,
I LIFT MY LAMP BESIDE THE GOLDEN DOOR!

We learned about the successes of just a few immigrants who have made the United States better with their ideas, their inventions, and their dreams. There are so many more whose stories are still being written.

If you feel inspired by these stories, look for more. Ask your grandparents, your neighbors, and your teachers what stories they know.

Then, start building your own story of success to share with the world!

Sources

In researching the amazing innovators included in this book, we read hundreds of profiles and interviews. If you would like to know more about the featured immigrant entrepreneurs, the bibliography is available upon request. These sources provide more information on each innovator, from their background to their company's challenges and triumphs.

For more information, visit duopressbooks.com.

Read More About Immigrants and Entrepreneurship

Carney, Elizabeth. *Ellis Island*. Washington, DC: National Geographic Kids, 2016.

Cohen, Ronnie, and Katherine Ellison. *Girl CEO: Priceless Advice from Trailblazing Women*. Georgia Rucker, illustrator. New York, NY: Downtown Books, 2018.

Howell, Sara. *Famous Immigrants and Their Stories*. New York, NY: Rosen Publishing, 2014.

Khan, Brooke. *Home of the Brave: 15 Immigrants Who Shaped U.S. History*. Berkeley, CA: Rockridge Press, 2019.

McConnell, Ericka, photographer, and Rachel Neumann, editor. *I Am Home: Portraits of Immigrant Teenagers*. Berkeley, CA: Parallax Press, 2018.

Wallace, Sandra Neil, and Rich Wallace. *First Generation: 36 Trailblazing Immigrants and Refugees Who Make America Great*. Agata Nowicka, illustrator. New York, NY: Little, Brown and Company, 2018.

AMBITION A strong desire to be successful.

APP A computer program.

ARCHITECTURE The art of designing buildings.

ASPIRE To desire to achieve something.

AUCTION A public space at which things are sold to the highest bidder.

CODE To put information into letters, numbers, or symbols so that it can be read by a computer.

COMPUTATION The act of calculating something.

CONCEPT An idea.

CONTRACTOR A person who is paid money to work or provide goods.

CORRUGATED Having a ridged or wavy surface.

CRYPTOGRAPHY Writing or reading secret codes.

DIGITAL Related to computer technology.

DISADVANTAGE Something causing difficulty or making a person less likely to succeed.

EMPOWER To give someone power or enable them.

ENGINEER A person who designs complicated products like machines or structures.

ENTREPRENEUR A person who starts a business.

FOSTER To help something grow.

FOUNDER A person who creates something new, like a business.

GRIT Courage or mental toughness.

HAVEN A safe place.

IMMIGRANT A person who comes to live in a foreign country.

INDUSTRY A group of businesses that create or provide the same type of product.

INFLUENTIAL Having power; being able to cause change.

INNOVATE To do something in a unique way.

INNOVATION The act or process of creating something unique.

INTERPRETER A person who translates what someone is saying into a different language.

LAUNCH To start something.

MERCHANDISE Goods that are bought or sold in business.

MIMIC To copy something.

MONITOR To watch something carefully.

NATIVE Born in a certain place.

PAVILION A building in a park that is used for special events.

PIONEER A person who helps create new things.

PITCH Things said by a person or group to make others want to buy or do something.

PORTFOLIO A collection of an artist's work.

POVERTY Being poor.

PROGRAMMING Creating computer programs.

PROTOTYPE The first model of something.

RADIATION A dangerous energy that is created by nuclear reactions.

REFINED Improved to be more exact.

REFUGEE A person who has fled a country because of violence or discrimination.

REGISTRY An official system or book for keeping a record of items; a list of gifts that a couple would like to receive when getting married.

RELIANT Needing something for support.

RENOVATION The process of improving something.

REPRESENTATIVE A person who acts or speaks for others.

RESIDENCY The period when a doctor trains at a hospital to become a specialist in a certain field of medicine.

RESOURCE Something that provides useful information.

RETAILER A business that sells products directly to customers.

REVOLUTIONARY Causing great change.

SMUGGLER Someone who illegally moves a person or thing from one country to another.

SOFTWARE Computer programs that have a specific function.

SPECIALIZE To concentrate on one specific area of study or business.

SYMBOLIC Representing an idea without the use of words.

TANGY Having a strong, sharp taste.

TRADITIONAL Describes the way of thinking or behavior of a certain group; following the tradition of a certain culture.

TRAILBLAZER A person who creates something new and makes it popular.

VISA A stamp in a passport that allows someone to enter or stay in a country.

VISIONARY Someone who has strong ideas or imagination about what can be done in the future.

Index

About the Author

Samantha Chagollan is an award-winning author and editor of a variety of children's fiction and nonfiction books. A native of Southern California, she grew up in Orange County and earned a bachelor's degree in literature from Humboldt State University in Arcata, California, where she focused her studies on multicultural literature and the Spanish language. Through these studies, she took a deeper dive into the heritage of her paternal grandparents and found a deep admiration for the determination and dedication it took for them to emigrate from Mexico to the United States in the 1920s. Without their sacrifices, she recognizes with deep appreciation that none of the successes of their children, grandchildren, and great grandchildren would have been possible. Samantha lives in Costa Mesa, California, with her husband Matt, and when she's not writing, she loves spending time with her dogs Charlie and Chloe, making art, and teaching yoga.

About the Illustrator

Calef Brown is the author and illustrator of 13 books for children including *Polkabats and Octopus Slacks: 14 Stories*; *Flamingos on the Roof: Poems and Paintings*, a *New York Times* bestseller; *The Ghostly Carousel*; and most recently, *Up Verses Down* (2019). He has also illustrated the work of a variety of authors, including James Thurber, Daniel Pinkwater, Edward Lear, and F. Scott Fitzgerald. Calef's illustrations have appeared in *Newsweek*, the *New Yorker*, *Rolling Stone*, *Time*, and many other publications, and he has created art for murals, packaging, and animation. He lives and works in Providence, Rhode Island.